Asteroids and Comets

William B. Rice

Consultant

JoBea Holt, Ph.D.
The Climate Project
Nashville, Tennessee

Publishing Credits

Dona Herweck Rice, *Editor-in-Chief*; Lee Aucoin, *Creative Director*; Don Tran, *Print Production Manager*; Timothy J. Bradley, *Illustration Manager*; Chris McIntyre, *Editorial Director*; James Anderson, *Associate Editor*; Jamey Acosta, *Associate Editor*; Jane Gould, *Editor*; Peter Balaskas, *Editorial Administrator*; Neri Garcia, *Senior Designer*; Stephanie Reid, *Photo Editor*; Rachelle Cracchiolo, M.S.Ed., *Publisher*

Image Credits

cover Antonova Elena/Shutterstock; p.1 Antonova Elena/Shutterstock; p.4 Shalygin/Shutterstock; p.5 Hemera Technologies/Abelstock; p.6 (background) NASA, (foreground) BrandonHot/Shutterstock; p.8 liquidlibrary/Jupiterimages; p.9 BSIP/Photo Researchers, Inc.; p.10 Argus/Shutterstock; p.11 Carmen Martínez Banús/iStockphoto; p.12 Pinchuk Alexey/Shutterstock; p.14 Walter G Arce/Shutterstock; p.15 (top) Pichugin Dmitry/Shutterstock, (bottom) Michael Gray/iStockphoto; p.16 magaliB/istockphoto; p.18 Clifford Mueller/iStockphoto; p.19 NASA; p.20 xjbxjhxm123/Shutterstock; p.21 (foreground) NASA/JPL-Caltech/T. Pyle (SSC); p.23 Robert Goode/Shutterstock; p.24 Vlue/Shutterstock; p.25 Newsom; p.26 Peter Miller/istockphoto; p.27 tpuerzer/istockphoto; p.28 Rocket400 Studio/Shutterstock; p.29 Karn Lowe; p.32 KRT/Newscom

Teacher Created Materials

5301 Oceanus Drive
Huntington Beach, CA 92649-1030
http://www.tcmpub.com
ISBN 978-1-4333-1424-7
©2011 Teacher Created Materials, Inc.
Reprinted 2013

Table of Contents

Amazing Space!

Space is full of amazing things. Just look up! You never know what you will find.

Asteroids

Are there rocks in space? You bet!
There are many of them. **Asteroids** are like
big rocks. Some are even like small planets!

Ceres

moon

Ceres is the biggest asteroid we know. See how big it is compared to the moon and Earth.

Asteroids are made of rock and a metal called iron.

Earth

Many asteroids move around the sun.
Some move in a **belt**. There is a belt
between Mars and Jupiter.

An asteroid

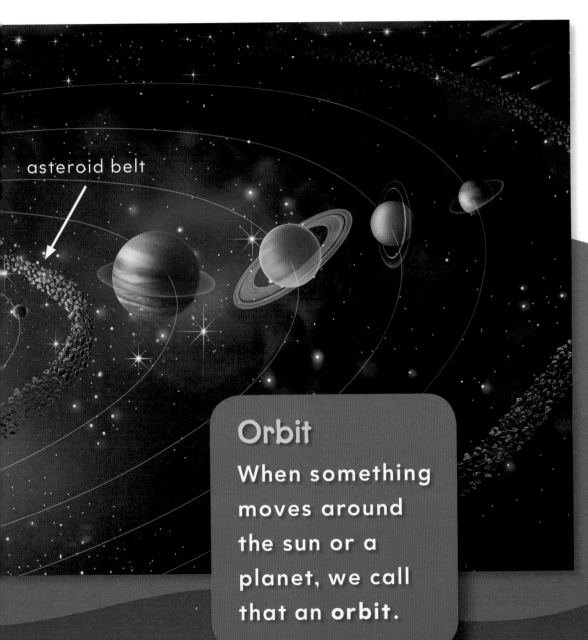

asteroid belt

Orbit

When something moves around the sun or a planet, we call that an **orbit**.

Some asteroids come close to Earth. They heat up when they do. They start to glow. We see a streak of light. This is called a **meteor**. It is also called a shooting star.

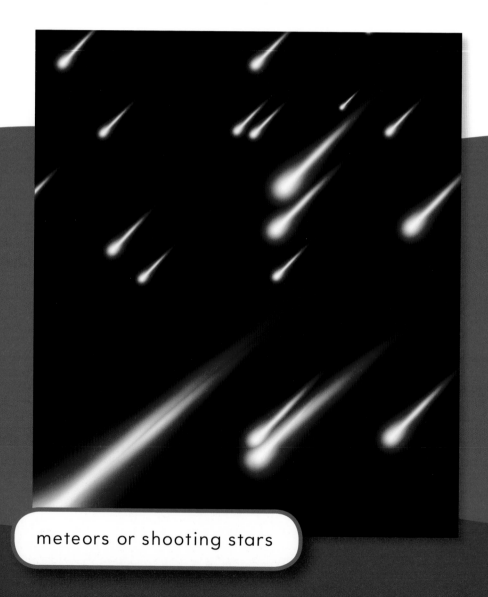

meteors or shooting stars

Telescopes can help us see objects in space. Use one to watch for meteors!

Many meteors burn up in the sky. But some hit Earth. They do not cause much trouble though. They are too small for that. But some meteors are huge! They can cause a lot of trouble.

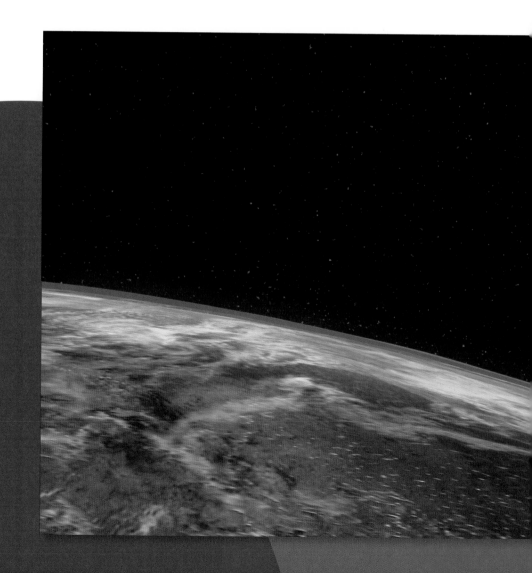

Asteroids may smash into each other. They can break into smaller bits. They may even smash into planets! Earth is a planet. Asteroids are called **meteorites** if they fall to Earth. Big meteorites can make holes in the planet.

This **crater** was made by a meteorite.

This big meteorite was found buried in the ground in Africa.

Fun Fact

Meteorites may be the reason why there are no more dinosaurs.

Comets

Comets orbit the sun. Most comets orbit far, far away. A comet may take a hundred years to go all the way around the sun.

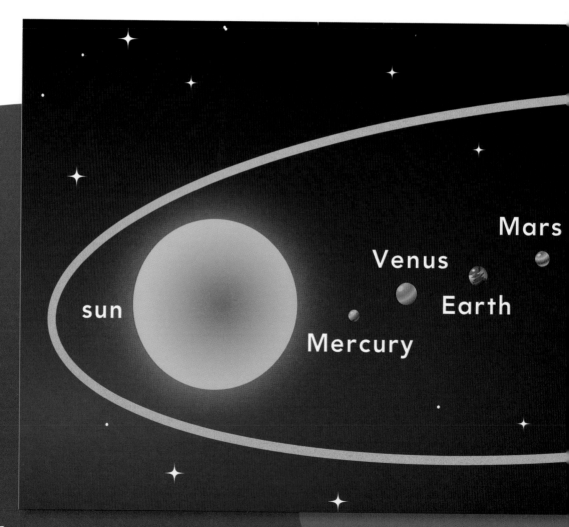

sun

Mercury

Venus

Earth

Mars

Some comets may take millions of years to go all the way around the sun!

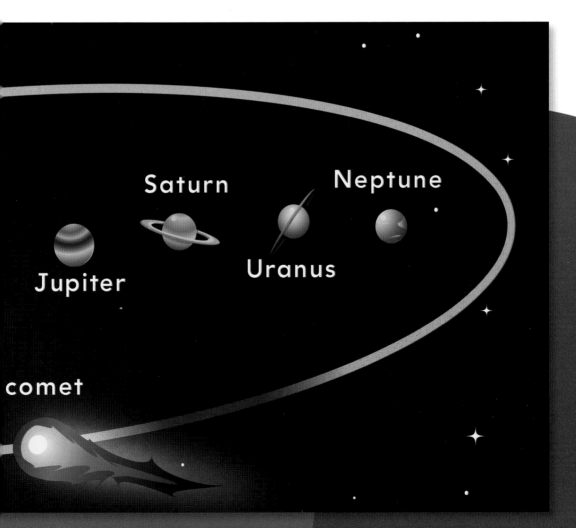

Comets are made of rock. They are made of ice and **gas**, too.

comet

comet

Comets are like big, dirty snowballs. They shoot off gas and dust when they get near the sun.

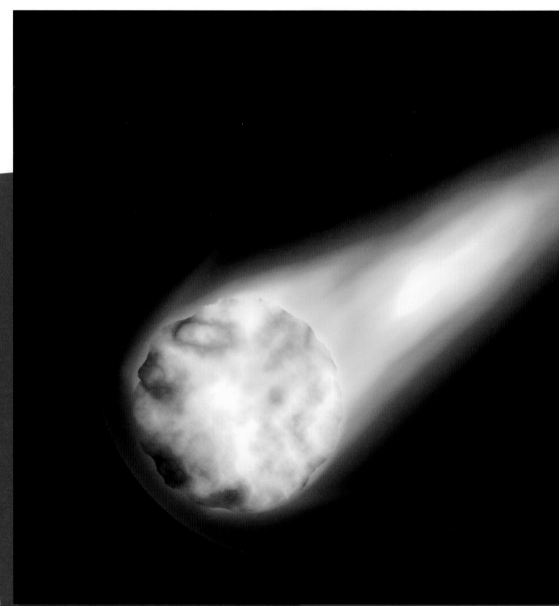

Comets come in many sizes. The smallest is about 100 meters wide.

The gas and dust make a long tail. The tail lights up in the sky. It always points away from the sun.

Fun Fact

The word *comet* comes from a Greek word that means "long hair." Can you tell why?

Some comets come close to Earth. We can see them in the sky. Earth may pass through the comet's path. Then we see a meteor shower!

meteor shower

Perseid Meteor Shower

We can see this famous meteor shower every August.

What Do You See?

Look up in the sky tonight. What will you see? Watch for meteors and comets! You never know when one will pass your way.

Goodbye, meteors and comets!

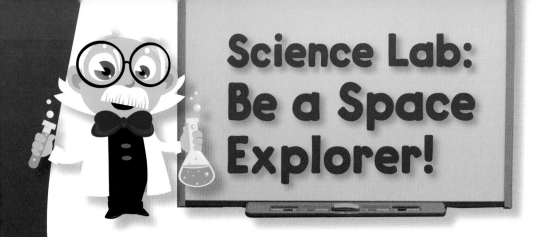

Science Lab: Be a Space Explorer!

Moons, asteroids, and comets are just some of the things that move around in space. Scientists study all these things. One way to learn about them is by watching them.

You can be a space explorer by watching the moon.

Materials:

- paper
- crayons or markers
- the moon at night

Procedure:

1. Take a piece of paper and draw seven boxes on it. Write the numbers 1 through 7 in the boxes, as shown.

2 After dark, go outside with a grownup and look up at the moon. What do you see?

3 Draw what you see in the first box on the paper.

4 At the same time on the next night, do the same thing. Draw what you see in the second box.

5 Do the same thing each night at the same time for seven nights.

6 After seven nights, look at all of your drawings. What do they show you about the moon?

Glossary

asteroids—large rocks traveling through space

belt—a band or strip that goes around in a circle

comets—balls of rock, ice, and gas that orbit the sun and have long tails near the sun

crater—a large hole or dent

gas—a state of matter that is not solid or liquid

meteorites—asteroids or other objects that land on Earth

meteors—asteroids or other objects that come close to Earth, heat up, and glow in the sky

orbit—to move in a circle or oval around something else

Index

A Scientist Today

Mae Jemison was an astronaut. She traveled into space to learn about everything you find there. She thinks that the best scientists are always asking questions. Today, Mae teaches students to be scientists.